ABOUT THE AUTHOR

Ronald L. Hoffman, M.D., is Medical Director of The Hoffman Center in New York City. A graduate of Albert Einstein College of Medicine, he is a Diplomate of the American College of Advancement in Medicine and The American Academy of Environmental Medicine. He is the author of *Lyme Disease* and *Natural Therapies for Mitral Valve Prolapse* (Keats Good Health Guides), *The Diet-Type Weight Loss Program, Seven Weeks to a Settled Stomach* and *Tired All the Time: How to Regain Your Lost Energy*. He also hosts "Health Talk," a daily radio program which is syndicated nationally.

The Natural Approach to
Attention
Deficit Disorder
(ADD)

Drug-free ways to treat
the roots of this
childhood epidemic

Ronald L. Hoffman, M.D.
Author of *Natural Therapies for Mitral Valve Prolapse*

KEATS PUBLISHING

LOS ANGELES

NTC/Contemporary Publishing Group

The Natural Approach to Attention Deficit Disorder (ADD) is not intended as medical advice. Its intent is solely informational and educational. Please consult a health professional should the need for one be indicated.

THE NATURAL APPROACH TO ATTENTION DEFICIT DISORDER (ADD)

ISBN: 0-87983-779-9

Printed in the United States of America

21 DIG/DIG   16 15

Contents

ADD/ADHD: AN ILLNESS OR A LABEL?

"They told me there was nothing that could be done," Jeanne lamented about her four-year-old child, "They told me I should consider institutionalizing him as a permanent option—we might just have to lock him up and throw away the key." Michael was alternately withdrawn and impossible, throwing tantrums over food, going ballistic at being touched, over-reacting to sounds. He seemed to have a limited attention span, was slow to develop normal skills, and was unable to engage in normal children's play activities for more than a few minutes at a time. In fact, he didn't interact very well with other children at all. He seemed distracted, uninterested.

Michael had been diagnosed by one psychiatrist as having ADD, attention deficit disorder. He'd been recommended for a course of Ritalin, the standard medication for this syndrome, but his parents were concerned about the effects of sustained, long-term medication. They were in despair, especially his mother, Jeanne, who had had Michael, her first and only child, at the age of 35. It seemed like a cruel stroke of fate to her.

Perhaps because she was a psychiatric social worker, she believed there might be possibilities for healing or improving his condition other than Ritalin, and she came to see me. We did extensive tests, prescribed a course of treatment, and a year later Jeanne reported to me that she had taken Michael for an evaluation by the disabilities office at his new school, and they had asked her, "Why are you bringing him in? He doesn't seem to need us." At the end of the kindergarten school year, Michael's teacher reported that he was a delight to have in class, and she sometimes held up Michael's behavior as a model to the other children. What happened? How could such a switch be possible? Were the psychiatrists wrong?

Michael was not too much of a behavioral problem in his visits to our clinic, but we have had other children come in and start rocketing around the office, pulling books off shelves, jumping on and off furniture, breaking the equipment. These were pretty strong young kids who could really turn the office upside down and sometimes required several patient and gentle staff members to manage them. Sean was one of these. His mother came to me almost in tears, telling me that he was prone to unbelievable tantrums and had caused a crisis at his day school of such proportions that they had had to send all the kids home. They had to clear the school just as they might have for an earthquake or a hurricane. When Sean wasn't having tantrums, he was fidgety, hyperactive, literally bouncing off the walls. He had been diagnosed by the psychiatric profession with a variation of the ADD syndrome called ADHD, attention deficit hyperactivity disorder. About 60 percent of children with ADD are also hyperactive. Sean had actually started taking the prescribed medication, Ritalin, but it didn't seem to be improving his behavior very much. With the start of medication, however, he lost his appetite, had difficulty falling asleep and complained of constant headaches. Please, she begged me, wasn't there anything I could do?

What's Happening to Our Children?
   ADD and ADHD would seem to be an epidemic sweeping the country. At the very least, they are labels being attached to an increasing number of children—upwards of a million in recent years—representing 3 to 5 percent of school-aged children. More and more children are being recommended for the standard medication, Ritalin (methylphenidate), a member of the amphetamine category of drugs. In some school districts, more than 7 percent of the children are receiving this treatment.
   The question is, are ADD and ADHD on the rise, is our awareness of them on the rise or are we trying to deal with children's behavior problems in a pharmaceutical way? Media controversy has been heating up on this subject, with everyone from the Scientologists to the editorial staff of the *Wall Street Journal* and the *Journal of the American Medical Association* writing with concern about possible Ritalin overuse. In 1993, a United Nations report estimated that the U.S. was producing and consuming five times more methylphenidate than all the people in the rest of the world combined. It's a fact that the amount of Ritalin sold annually has been increasing at an

astounding rate—prescriptions have doubled in the past five years, and the amount produced has increased sixfold. High school students have been buying the pills from classmates, crushing them and snorting for a quick high. Drug manufacturers are cashing in on a bonanza and may be indulging in some questionable promotional practices. For example, they are financial contributors to a national support group called CHAADD, Children and Adults with ADD, which is an advocate for the use of Ritalin.

Diagnosis Fads: The Label Is Not a Disease

The real controversy about ADD is whether we are seeing a tendency to label all aberrant behavior as ADD, from the bright kid who is a little bit of a pain in the neck and acts up in class, to the quiet child who seems distracted and uninterested in school, to the child who may be suffering from some real physical sensations that he doesn't understand and can't control. We may also be looking at a peculiar phenomenon of medical understanding or misunderstanding similar to the "cholesterol fad." It's clear that some people are affected by cholesterol levels in their blood in a major way, but over the past few decades we've gone from nonrecognition of the problem to recognition that cholesterol is a health factor, to hyperviligance over cholesterol involving diet changes and even drugs, while ignoring other risk factors for cardiovascular disease.

Similarly, true ADD and ADHD are documented syndromes, and the people who have studied these have done us a service in identifying a hard-core group of kids with clear problems. Unfortunately, the pendulum now has swung so this has become a vogue diagnosis that covers a multitude of different behavior patterns which may have a number of distinct causes. The notion of applying the same therapeutic drug to all children with behavior problems is an abdication of responsibility.

As early as 1988, the *Journal of the American Medical Association* sounded a clarion call demanding more careful and restrictive diagnosis to establish true ADD and ADHD. An editorial questioned whether the increase in medication use "represents a return to an antiquated, simplistic approach that views all school and behavioral problems as one," and suggests that "it would be irresponsible to simply use methylphenidate as a panacea for all difficulties a child might experience in school;

the agent is valuable for the treatment of particular target symptoms, not as some magical potion to wash away all life's difficulties."[1] Remarkably, this is not the voice of alternative holistic medicine—it's the medical establishment. We might go even further and question whether even a clear diagnosis of ADD or ADHD necessarily warrants the automatic prescription of Ritalin or similar drugs. In this booklet, we'll take a closer look at ADD and ADHD-type behavior, at some of the multiple underlying causative factors and at therapies that can bypass the Ritalin bandwagon, but first let's consider Ritalin and other stimulant drug therapies.

DRUG THERAPY: A SIMPLE SOLUTION FOR A COMPLEX PROBLEM

The most commonly prescribed medication for ADD or ADHD is Ritalin (methylphenidate), which is a stimulant related to the amphetamine family of drugs. One of the myths about Ritalin is that if administering a stimulant to a hyperactive child calms him down, that proves that he had ADHD. The fact is, stimulants like Ritalin will increase the attention span and the ability to focus on a task in "normal" children and adults as well. A child who is distracted and physically active will not be so much "calmed down" by Ritalin as simply rendered more able to focus on one activity at a time, including "sit-down" activities. What the drug does in children with ADD and ADHD is physiologically push them into the normal range of behavior. What it does not do is address the underlying problems that may have caused the abnormal behavior.

Nor does Ritalin provide a cure or permanent correction of ADD or ADHD. While some children seem to improve with puberty, 80 percent of children retain some symptoms at the end of eight years despite drug treatments and behavioral modifications. This suggests that drugs don't really change the underlying problems. And Ritalin doesn't work for everyone. Some children respond to the medications successfully with greatly improved behavior that they and their parents are happy with, but others don't. Many get either an imperfect resolution of their problems or have troublesome side effects. By using Ritalin in many instances we may be masking other types of problems that can be resolved in a manner less potentially hazardous. Some of the potential side effects of Ritalin include reduced appetite, trouble in falling asleep, headaches, tearfulness and a decrease in rate of growth. In some children Ritalin can cause tics, especially when there is a family history of tics.

When Ritalin doesn't seem to work or the side effects are troubling, doctors try other stimulant drugs such as Dexedrine and Cylert. These have side effects even more frequently. Those of Dexedrine are similar to Ritalin, while Cylert can also affect blood pressure, heart rate and cause inflammation of the liver. Tricyclic antidepressants are also used, such as Norpramin, Pamelor and Tofranil, which have their own side effects, such as tiredness, dry mouth, heart problems, and constipation. (I see many children with ADD and ADHD who suffer from severe constipation with or without the drugs.) Antihypertensive drugs such as Catapres and Tenex are often given to children who have tics as well as ADD or ADHD, and they are given in combination with the stimulants. Side effects include sedation, headaches, nausea, dry mouth and constipation, and the child's blood pressure and heart rate have to be carefully monitored to identify any possible drug-induced abnormalities.

There is another concern about using these drugs. Amphetamine-family drugs have a definite abusive-addictive potential, and this includes Ritalin. Kids who get used to taking a drug every day and feel they can't get going in the morning without it, may start to think, "Hey, this stuff really works, really gets my head together, why not take some more? Why not try some Dexedrine or methamphetamine and see what that's like?" And in fact there are kids who take Ritalin tablets sold on the street, grind them up and snort them up their noses. When taken that way it produces a drug high quite different from the effects of taking a carefully metered dosage. Thus the danger is that familiarity with Ritalin may lead to dangerous drug experimentation.

The fact is, the drugs used to treat ADD/ADHD are powerful, the side effects are not negligible and the drugs should not be casually used. However, the widespread prescribing of these drugs indicates that we are involved in an unprecedented experiment with our children's health. We could be doing some good for some children, but this is also a gamble. We need to make sure that the risks are balanced by the benefits. Unfortunately, there are many cases where Ritalin is prescribed unnecessarily and to the detriment of the child, because a school, parents or doctors are looking for a quick fix. It's become expedient to address a complex problem with a one-size-fits-all drug. Rather, we should look at the individuality of each child, explore in detail the possible causes of ADD or ADHD-type behavior and address those with specific therapies. If we can use natural therapies as an end run around the prescription for Ritalin or other medication, I think we should do it. Let's look at some of the possible causes and alternative therapies for ADD and ADHD.

WHY CHILDREN HAVE PROBLEMS

Typically, parents will come to my office with a child who has already received a diagnosis of ADD or ADHD. They feel tremendous pressure to do something to help their child but are either unhappy about the drug prescription they are being offered or they are already aware that there are alternative models that may explain their child's behavior. I tell them their children are not sick because they've been diagnosed with ADHD, but they have these symptoms because there is some underlying health problem. Our job is to identify the problem or problems and treat them.

The most common physical issues are problems with sugar metabolism (hypoglycemia), allergies, food reactions, chemical sensitivities and individual nutritional deficiencies. There may be multiple overlapping causal factors plus possible environmental or cultural influences. A certain number of children misdiagnosed with ADD or ADHD turn out to have learning disabilities, such as dyslexia, or simply individual learning styles that are not the cultural norm. Or they may suffer from overwhelming psychological pressures that are not being addressed. Most of the children I see, however, have real physical problems that are causing their abnormal behavior.

It's interesting to note that the latest research on autism, an even more profound disturbance of mental function and behavior, has uncovered a similar pattern of multiple interlocking physiological abnormalities, many of which are treatable through nutrient and allergy analysis and therapy. The new theory is that ADD and autism may be at different locations on the same continuum, representing different expressions of some of the same underlying problems. In a holistic model, the same causes may result in two different expressions. For example, Crohn's disease and ulcerative colitis are considered two distinct medical entities, yet both may be caused by high sugar diets and food allergies.

What's remarkable is that striking recoveries have been achieved with autistic children who have a condition that's generally considered fundamental, intractable and hard-wired into the brain. The autism research offers not only great hope but practical approaches to treating ADD and ADHD. This has very encouraging implications for those kids who have a less profound disorder, such as ADD or ADHD-type behavior, since they are even more malleable in terms of their ability to learn and change. I frequently see a fairly simple dietary intervention—such as cutting out junk food, sugar and refined and processed foods and introducing whole foods without preservatives or additives—begin to cause significant behavioral improvements in children. This is why I usually start my examination of a child by asking the parent about the child's diet. We then go on to a thorough physical examination involving allergy testing and nutritional analysis through blood tests. To help understand how such things as food reactions and allergies can cause such profound behavioral changes in children, we should perhaps recall how different a child's experience of the world is from our own.

A CHILD'S SENSORY WORLD

Suppose you find yourself in the midst of hay fever season and you have to go to work but you're feeling miserable.

You're sniffling, you have a headache, a kind of a throbbing, stuffed-up feeling. How efficient do you feel in your mental functions when you have an intense allergy attack like this? Not very. Nevertheless, you've had 20 to 30 or more years to train your super-ego to help you ignore your bodily symptoms and take care of business. As an adult you have a highly developed super-ego in the Freudian sense. This is the part of the personality that tells you how you *should* behave, what you *must* do. You tell yourself, "I may not be feeling well, but I've got to take care of this, got to show up." You've learned self-discipline, you have a fully formed ego, an intact personality. You have experience in functioning even when you're not at your best, and you have the perspective to know this is only temporary. You still feel poorly, so you may be a little more nervous, snappish and testy, but you tough it out for the day. Or you may even decide to pack it in after a few hours, go home early, cancel your appointments and put the stack of work aside until tomorrow.

By contrast, children who experience powerful reactions of allergy, food intolerance or environmental toxicity have no internal resources to manage the miserable sensations. Their identities are still unformed and fluid, their personality structures are fragile, they have no years of practice in self-discipline. They may not ever have experienced consistent mental clarity so may not have the skills to rise above the murky haze in which they find themselves when beset with internal toxins or allergies.

The fact is that a child has a much more vulnerable sensory experience of the external and internal world than an adult. Children have a great deal more distractibility, especially as they experience tiredness and unpleasant physical sensations as they move away from a state of physical well-being. To the extent that allergies or food reactions may push them into uncomfortable physical states, this may affect their ability to concentrate, be attentive, or simply sit at rest comfortably.

Most of us remember how vivid and dramatic everyday experience could be when we were children, how powerful were the tastes of foods we loved or hated, how different was our very sense of time, so that a car ride our parents thought was no big deal seemed endless to us. We may feel nostalgic about childhood experience, but it had its down side as well. For an adult with a food allergy, eating a tomato may cause stomach upset or a headache, while the same food could send a child into an apparently inexplicable rage reaction. This is worth remembering as we look at some of the specific models of processes that can throw a child's sensory experience and behavior out of balance.

THE SUGAR/HYPOGLYCEMIA CONNECTION

Most kids are natural sugar junkies, going wild over candy, cake, ice cream, cookies and so on. It's an ingrained part of our culture. There are fairy tales about candy lands and gingerbread houses, we celebrate birthdays with cake and ice cream, we celebrate holidays with special kinds of sweets. For most children highly sweetened soda pop is the order of the day except among those whose parents think that fruit juice, laden with natural sugar, is a better choice. Some parents try to fight the sugar monster, but often feel it's a losing battle. Beyond sugar itself, children love to fill up on high-carbohydrate foods that quickly convert to a sugar called glucose in the bloodstream. Pizza, sugared high-carbohydrate breakfast cereals, bread, rice, french fries and spaghetti are common dietary staples among the young.

Most children survive the sugar onslaught without serious behavior problems, but a smaller percentage of children may be susceptible to powerful mood swings, physiological sensations and behavioral reactions as a result of sugar-laden and high-carbohydrate foods. A common scenario is that of the child who eats a poor breakfast, such as a sugared cereal or a doughnut; later in the morning he or she can't concentrate or pay attention to the teacher. Another example is when a child seems to crave bread, pasta or sweets and then goes ballistic, bouncing off the walls before suddenly crashing with tears and stomach upset.

How does this happen? When we eat sugar and carbohydrates, they are quickly converted to glucose in the bloodstream—usually in a matter of minutes. The high glucose levels then signal the body to produce massive amounts of insulin in order to process the glucose and reduce the blood sugar levels. The flood of insulin results in a bottoming out of the blood sugar to a depressed, abnormally low level. This low level of blood sugar is called hypoglycemia and is characterized by weakness, fatigue and spaciness. It's a dangerous condition that could lead to fainting or coma, so the body reacts by releasing stimulant hormones from the adrenal glands, including adrenaline. These are the same hormones that are released in the so-called "fight or flight" reaction to danger. They cause blood vessels to constrict, the heart rate to go up and the extremities to become cold and numb. The autonomic nervous system, which manages the unconscious bodily processes such as digestion and circulation, goes on hyperalert. This is accompanied by a jittery, breathless feeling. Muscles become taut and poised for action.

In adults, this reaction can be so powerful that it can cause a panic attack. People who are having a panic attack experience such frightening sensations that they often check themselves into emergency rooms, thinking they are having a heart attack. For some children, riding this roller coaster of sensation from a sugar rush to bottoming out to an adrenaline rush, can be an overwhelming experience. They can go literally berserk.

What's more, children appear to have a radically different response to sugar than adults. A recent study compared children's and adults' response to a sugar dose, measuring blood glucose and adrenaline every half-hour for five hours. Blood sugar levels remained in the normal range in both adults and children, but the adrenaline levels in the children were 10 times higher than normal up to five hours after the sugar dose. The kids were experiencing a major hormonal wallop.

Concern over this process was the basis of one of the earliest approaches to children's behavior problems, and studies were performed beginning in the 1970s that seemed to show some correlation between sugar and behavior. This is a controversial issue, and recent medical opinion has strongly discounted the sugar connection. Studies don't seem to support a universal effect of sugar on behavior. But a recent article in the *Journal of the American Medical Association* suggested that what we may need to do is look at subsets of kids who are susceptible to ADD or ADHD and examine their reactions to sugar.[3]

As a practicing physician, I see this controversy from a different perspective. The fact is, kids who are normal, who may not be affected by sugar, don't come to my office. I see the kids who have problems, and their parents tend to report that the kids get worse with sugar in their diets and better with sugar elimination. This may to some extent be the result of parental expectations, but there are a lot of therapies that don't work with these children, despite the placebo effect. If sugar elimination has a placebo effect, it's a very strong one. If the behavior improvement is based on parental expectations, let them keep expecting!

Another way in which a high-sugar, high-carbohydrate diet may indirectly cause behavioral problems is by promoting an overgrowth of yeast in a child's digestive tract. Varieties of yeast such as *Candida albicans* can grow in the digestive tract and cause disturbances in immune functioning as well as a condition called "leaky gut" in which more allergic substances and toxins are absorbed into the body.

I've observed significant improvement in children's behavior when they go off junk food, cut out sugar-rich and sweetened foods, high-carbohydrate foods and processed and refined foods in general, which are also packed with preservatives, food colorings and flavorings. It's important to be careful with the high-carbohydrate processed foods like breads, cereals, pastas, potatoes and processed grains, as well as "natural" snacks like dried fruit, granola bars and fruit drinks, since all these can send blood sugar rocketing and send a child off on the hypoglycemic roller coaster ride.

THE ALLERGY CONNECTION

Seven-year-old David's mother explained to me that he seemed obsessed with pizza. Whenever they went out, that's all he'd want to eat; whenever they would order in, he wanted pizza. Every day he'd ask if they could have pizza, and he wanted enough so that there would be leftovers in the refrigerator. She didn't really indulge him that much, but did sometimes have to give in. David would sit down and put away quite a few pizza slices, but instead of seeming satisfied, he'd wander off in a fog, irritable and distracted. If they were in a restaurant, he'd get up and mill around; there was no way to keep him in his seat. By the time they got home, he'd often complain of a headache and stomachache, and would finally sit in a kind of stupor, apparently profoundly depressed. But the next day he'd be demanding pizza again.

When I saw David in my office, we tested him for allergies and found strong reactions to wheat, dairy products and tomatoes—the main ingredients of pizza. David's pattern isn't unusual. I've seen other children go through similar craving, bingeing, and crashing behavior with bread, ice cream, popcorn or corn chips, peanut butter, chocolate and fruit juices. It's almost like an addiction/withdrawal cycle.

The fact is, many children respond with striking behavioral changes to things they eat and breathe. It is increasingly recognized that allergies, especially food allergies and food intolerances, may be a significant factor in many children diagnosed with ADD and ADHD. One of the principal researchers and educators in this area is Dr. Doris J. Rapp, an allergist and former clinical professor of pediatrics at the State University of New York at Buffalo. Dr. Rapp has published a number of books on this subject, such as the informative *Is This Your Child?*, and has performed an invaluable service in educating both the public and other medical professionals about this issue.

Dr. Rapp points out a fascinating group of physical characteristics common among children with allergies, including red cheeks, red ears or ear lobes, dark or red circles or wrinkles under the eyes, and a horizontal crease in the nose that develops from what she calls the "allergic salute," when a child with a runny nose rubs his nose upward with the heel of his hand. Other physical symptoms include diarrhea or constipation, excessive drooling or perspiration, recurring ear infections, coughing or asthma, headaches, muscle aches and intestinal complaints.

These physical symptoms are accompanied by behavior problems. Infants tend to have feeding and sleep problems, screaming, rocking or head-banging behavior and resist cuddling. Toddlers and young children may throw tantrums, become hyperactive, do a lot of hitting or spitting. As they grow older, they may behave erratically in learning or writing, may seem to have trouble remembering or concentrating, may appear withdrawn, tired, irritable or sad.

One troublesome marker of possible allergies in your child is chronic ear infections or ear pain. Allergies can cause ear infections both by interfering with the normal immune response and by physically constricting the Eustachian tubes and preventing the proper drainage of fluid from the ears. The trapped mucus provides an ideal culture medium for bacterial growth. Chronic ear infections can become an additional complicating factor if they inspire pediatricians to prescribe frequent courses of antibiotics. Excessive antibiotic use can disrupt the normal balance of beneficial bacteria in the intestines. This can result in yeast infections and other intestinal reactions, such as "leaky gut," that can increase a child's absorption of allergic or toxic substances.

Allergies and the Brain

An allergic person's immune system reacts to a common substance such as pollen or milk as if it were a dangerous disease-causing invader such as a virus or bacteria. The substance that causes this unneeded immune response is called an allergen. In this immune reaction, the body releases a whole array of cellular and chemical agents that may directly attack the allergen or may cue reactions that will help the body get rid of it. One of the principal immune agents is called histamine; this is the biochemical messenger that causes noses to run, eyes to water and blood vessels to constrict. People who have severe immune reactions can experience such a release of histamine that their bronchial passages completely close up, causing suffocation.

Our new understanding of the immune system and how it overlaps with the nervous system goes a long way toward explaining the powerful effects allergies can have on a child's behavior and state of mind. If you look at the body on the biochemical level, it's really not clear where the immune system leaves off and the nervous system begins. Both sense and process information and react in many cases automatically. Both rely on biochemical messengers for much of their functioning. Much of the activity of the brain is regulated not simply by the passing of impulses from one nerve cell to the next, but by messenger chemicals called neurotransmitters. These include chemicals like dopamine and serotonin, which have a profound effect on the functioning of the brain. Inadequate supplies or imperfect pathways for these neurotransmitters can cause profound mental disturbances, such as schizophrenia.

It turns out that some of these neurotransmitters can directly regulate the immune system and that some biochemicals released by the immune system can directly affect the brain as well, functioning as neurotransmitters. This is why if your body is mounting an immune response to a cold, the flu or an allergen, you may have difficulty concentrating, thinking, paying attention. Your brain is getting powerful subliminal signals that what you really should do is curl up in bed and let the immune system do its work.

In fact, there are pathways in the brain that react directly to histamines, which are a principal by-product of the allergic response. Histamine affects brain function just as do other classic neurotransmitters such as serotonin and dopamine. There are histamine receptors in all parts of the brain, but they are particularly concentrated in the limbic system, which is the part of the brain that is the seat of mood and emotion. Researchers have even speculated that new medications could be developed to treat mental disease, including schizophrenia, by blocking the histamine pathways. The implication of all this, of course, is that allergic reactions may directly influence brain function in children and may have a profound effect on their behavior and mental state.

Researcher Abram Hoffer coined the term "brain allergy" to describe this kind of allergic effect on children. People tend to think of allergy as something that affects the skin, mucous membranes or the digestive tract, producing a rash on the skin, a runny nose, wheezing or an upset stomach. Even allergists think this way. Hoffer and others proposed that some allergies can cause a brain reaction because histamine, the chemical substance produced in an allergic reaction, is also a neurotransmitter.[4]

One thing we can do to find out if a child may have a brain allergy is to give histamine drops under the tongue or by histamine injection and observe the child's behavior. If it changes markedly—if the child becomes either spacey or hyperactive—we can take this one step further and ask, what allergen is triggering the histamine release in this child?

Allergy, Intolerance and Other Food Reactions

What we've just described is only one way that a substance a child eats or inhales can affect behavior through a classic allergic pathway. There are other powerful ways that foods can affect behavior that are not strictly allergic. We tend to lump many food reactions together under the term allergies when not all are classic immune reactions. A food intolerance, for example, is a genetic glitch or peculiarity in body chemistry or enzyme activity that prevents normal digestion or utilization of some types of foods. The immune system isn't involved.

True food allergies are fairly rare, though they can cause life-threatening reactions. When it comes to children's behavioral responses, the distinction between allergies and intolerances gets fairly blurred because the symptoms and the effects are so much alike. We'll generally use the term food allergy or simply food reaction to refer to both allergies and intolerances here, and will describe some possible food-based reactions other than allergies below.

How to Identify Food Allergies and Reactions
Some food reactions are fairly easy to identify, but others are not. Some can be very hard to pin down. They may occur several hours after a child eats, may trigger a whole range of symptoms, and wax and wane. If the child is reactive to several foods, this can complicate the issue further.

There are several ways a doctor can test for classic food allergies. One is by administering a blood test called the RAST. The RAST test measures the levels of immunoglobulins in the blood, which contain antibodies to allergic substances. The standard RAST test, which is the only RAST test that many allergists offer, measures levels of immunoglobulin E (IgE) and will confirm obvious allergies, especially to inhaled substances like cat dander or dust that result in itching, swollen eyes or wheezing. Many food allergies are more subtle, subliminal, or delayed in effect, however, and will not show up on the standard IgE RAST. When we suspect a food allergy, we often give an additional RAST test for IgG, a different immunoglobulin. We commonly see children in our office who test negative for IgE but strongly positive for IgG, which usually correlates with the parents' observations.

The second principal method of identifying allergies is with a skin provocation test. This involves injecting a concentrated amount of a possible allergic substance just under the skin or placing a drop of extract on a "scratched" area of the skin. If the treated area reddens, itches, or develops a welt, it usually signifies an allergy to the substance. This is a bit of a trial and error process; we start with some common allergens and just work our way through a list of possible offenders. The provocation test often reveals allergies that don't show up in a RAST test, especially if a food has a direct neurological effect instead of going through the immune or allergy pathways and inducing a histamine reaction. (More later on neurotoxic food components, which aren't strictly allergies.)

In small children or when cooperation is a problem, we place a drop of the concentrate under the tongue and observe the child for physical or behavioral changes. A challenge with the substance, a provocation, can sometimes directly evoke a symptom, such as a change in pulse rate, a change in handwriting or a behavior change. One common method is to ask the child to print his or her name before the test and again after the provocation since children can respond to allergic substances with drastic impairment of their ability to write. I've seen children who react dramatically to this test—they become irritable, restless, or completely out of control.

These tests are helpful, but they do not identify all food allergies, which can be very elusive. The one sure-fire way to find out if a child is allergic or reactive to a food is to eliminate it from his or her diet. This means eliminating not only the obvious foods, such as milk or cheese, but all foods that may contain some extract or processed version of dairy such as baked goods made with milk, etc. The goal is to completely eliminate all sources and traces of the food. After a short period, usually of four days, the food is reintroduced, often in a substantial amount for several meals in a row or until symptoms recur.

If the eliminated food is a problem when reintroduced, behavioral or physical symptoms may reappear in a marked and obvious manner since the child has "de-adapted" to the offending food. The elimination diet is the ultimate reference and will reveal problem foods that haven't shown up either in a RAST test or by provocation. Reactions to the reintroduction of problem foods can be profound, so it's best to get some guidance from a physician if you are going to work with elimination diets. In some cases, the foods should be reintroduced in very small amounts. Of course, you may see such dramatic improvement that you decide not to reintroduce the problem food at all.

When children are sensitive to several foods, it can be tough to get clear results even from the elimination diet because it's hard to get a clear baseline when the child isn't reacting to something. In these cases, we try a multiple elimination diet, providing a few simple foods that are rarely allergenic, along with nonallergenic nutritional support such as UltraCare powdered drink. We then reintroduce suspect foods one at a time and eliminate any that cause a reaction.

Treating Allergies

Food allergies might seem to be the easiest to treat—you just avoid the problem food, right? But that's not always so easy. In this day of highly processed foods, we don't always know what has been used in the preparation of a dish from additives to processed components. Food manufacturers and restaurants commonly use many potentially allergy-producing foods in preparing a product. Many food products contain wheat flour, eggs or milk. You would think you could identify problem foods by reading the labels, but it's not always possible. Casein, a milk protein, is often used in breads, sauces and baked goods even when milk is not listed as an ingredient. Peanut allergy is very common, and peanut oil is used in many commercial baked goods, potato chips and candies. Corn products, especially, such as cornstarch, corn syrup and corn oil, are so pervasive that they can be found in nearly every kind of prepared or processed food, and many aren't always listed as such on product labels.

If we do want to eliminate a lot of foods because of multiple allergies—such as to wheat, corn and dairy—we may find it hard to provide a child with a consistent, nutritionally rich, calorie-dense diet. We may find that a child simply has trouble thriving when all allergic foods are eliminated. One way to help is to plug in the nutritional gaps with a hypoallergenic product like the UltraCare drink. But there are other ways to help children with multiple allergies or reactions to common foods and other allergens.

Provocation/neutralization can help desensitize a child to single allergens, and it is especially useful with allergens that are difficult to avoid, such as dust or grass pollen. We give an injection or drop of the concentrated allergen beneath the tongue, wait 7 to 10 minutes and then give diluted drops of the same concentrate. If there is still a reaction, we wait again and continue giving the concentrate in progressively greater dilutions until we arrive at a dilution that causes no reaction. This is the dosage we can then use to neutralize the allergic response.

A child can take the drops once or twice daily at home to protect against inadvertent exposure to the allergen. By gradually increasing the doses over a long period of time we can sometimes effectively eliminate sensitivity to the substance. This works very well for some, but children vary greatly in how they respond and some never get completely desensitized. Nevertheless, some parents find this method very helpful in managing reactions to inhaled allergens, yeast, or even to the biochemical products of an immune reaction like histamine.

Conventional allergists don't believe you can be desensitized to food allergies in this way, but many environmental physicians have had good success with neutralizing food reactions. We recently treated a child with severe corn allergies who has improved greatly with an elimination diet; he's calmer, less fidgety, more centered and not ruled by tremendous explosions of energy. Corn by-products are very difficult to completely eliminate, especially when a child is likely to eat snacks and processed foods at school and with friends. However, neutralization drops are helping this child negotiate these inadvertent challenges to his system.

A New Approach to Allergy Treatment

Sherry brought in two sons one day, Matt and Evan, four and six years old. They had both been diagnosed with ADD and both were asthmatic, with frequent upper-respiratory problems. Neither had been breast-fed, so their immune systems had not received the benefits of their mother's immune conditioning. Instead, they had gotten an early exposure to cow's milk, which often sets children up for allergy, and in fact they had both suffered from infant colic. Evan was so prone to ear infections that his pediatrician had recommended the operation called myringotomy, which opens up the ear tubes so fluid will drain. Matt was having trouble in his preschool and Evan in first grade, partly because they were frequently home sick and partly because they didn't seem to engage fully when they were in school. Their teachers remarked on their poor attention spans, and Sherry was urged to put Evan on Ritalin.

All the symptoms Sherry described to me suggested allergies, and when we tested the boys we found they not only had inhalant allergies but a whole panoply of food allergies. Stool tests indicated they had yeast overgrowth as well. This was especially understandable in Evan's case, since he had had so many antibiotic treatments for his ear infections.

We did get the children onto a diet that eliminated many foods and seemed to reduce their asthmatic symptoms and absences from school. Their schoolwork and concentration improved, and the examining psychologist decided that Ritalin was no longer necessary. Sherry and her husband Ron were happy and relieved.

Unfortunately, the boys' diets were an onerous chore for both parents to manage. The diets were similar, since the two boys had some allergies in common, but they weren't exactly the same. For Matt, we eliminated eggs, wheat, milk, tomatoes and citrus fruit and juice; for Evan, we eliminated eggs, wheat, corn and apples. Evan was allergic to tree pollen as well. We also put them both on a candida diet with restricted sugar. They clearly were doing better, but it was a huge hassle for their parents to keep their diets sorted out. On top of this, there would be setbacks when they went to birthday parties or play dates or visited their grandparents' house. Other parents couldn't always remember the boys' needs, and their grandparents somehow never accepted their diet limitations.

What's worse, while their symptoms were much improved over time, it seemed that they weren't thriving. They were healthy but very thin, and over the course of the year Evan gained only two pounds, way below normal, which suggested that his diet was too restricted nutritionally.

At this point, we employed EPD, an allergy desensitization technique pioneered in England, which is often effective in broadly desensitizing children to multiple allergies. EPD, or enzyme-potentiated desensitization, has been shown in studies of kids with ADHD and food reactions to greatly increase tolerance to a wide range of provoking foods and to effectively control food-provoked hyperactive behavior.[5] As a result, Matt and Evan are now broadening their diet, successfully eating some of the foods they were reacting to before, and doing so safely without any worsening of their asthmatic or behavioral symptoms. EPD appears to be a potentially invaluable therapeutic approach for enabling allergic kids to live in the real world.

Neurotoxins and Other Food Reactions

Jamal's parents had an air of hopelessness when they brought him to see me. Jamal, at four years old, didn't behave like a normal, active child. He seemed listless and lethargic, uninterested in his surroundings. His parents explained that he wasn't developing normal language and motor skills, and that their doctor had sent them to a neurologist who had sent them to a psychologist, who had handed them an ADD diagnosis. Jamal's mother mentioned that he was extremely finicky about his eating, to the point of going on strike if she insisted on giving him anything other than what he wanted. I asked "What's he eating?" And his mother told me, "He has pancakes for breakfast, bread and butter for lunch, eats pretzels throughout the day, and spaghetti for dinner, but without tomato sauce, just butter and salt. He doesn't really like meat." It turned out Jamal was eating wheat products with every meal as well as in between, not getting much protein. He was also perpetually constipated.

This pattern was a red flag for a kind of food reaction that is not really an allergy because there is no immune reaction, but it can be just as troubling. In fact, wheat is one of the most common causes of food reactions. Some children are profoundly sensitive to all wheat products. In their systems, improperly digested wheat fragments that pass into their bloodstream appear to mimic powerful chemical neurotransmitters that are similar to opium. There are proteins called peptides, particularly in wheat, that can attach to the opiate receptors in the brain. When children eat wheat products, these neurotoxins cause them to feel tired, lethargic, spacey and distracted. They may experience intestinal bloating and often suffer from constipation, a common side effect of opiates. Many of these children also develop food cravings for the very offending substance that gets them "stoned," and this can lead to binge eating.

I explained this to Jamal's parents. I said that he was probably suffering from carbohydrate overload and hypoglycemia from eating so much bread and pasta, plus he was experiencing the neurotoxic effect of the wheat particles. I mentioned that his constipation was a strong indicator of the opiate-like neurotoxins and suggested that the first thing to try to help him would be to eliminate all wheat and wheat products from his diet.

His mother resisted trying to change Jamal's diet and asked if I could offer any evidence that wheat was the problem because, as she told me, "It's going to start World War III if we have to eliminate all these foods—that's all he'll eat!" I suggested just trying it to see if it would help, but when she swore she couldn't, I offered to do some tests to establish whether wheat was causing Jamal's problems.

We did a novel test called the organic acids test, which reveals the presence of peptides in the urine, which can be derived from wheat protein (gliadin) as well as from milk and meat proteins. Sure enough, Jamal showed a high peptide level, and his mother finally agreed to try the elimination diet. I told her that my experience has been that when you change a child's diet in a case like this the child will go through withdrawal, and for a couple of days there can be a real contest of wills. But kids have a pretty strong survival instinct and they're not going to starve themselves on account of a diet change if offered good tasty food of a different type. There was a bit of a rough transition period with Jamal, but his mother was eventually able to get him off the wheat. She substituted rice for a carbohydrate and increased the protein in his diet with beans and meat.

The most dramatic response was that Jamal quickly recovered from his severe constipation and began having completely normal bowel movements. His behavior started to improve as well; he became much more attentive to his surroundings and more physically active. He still exhibited some ADD-like behavior, but was much improved since he was no longer intoxicated by the wheat neurotoxins throughout the day.

Leaky Gut Syndrome

Leaky gut syndrome is a double risk for some children with ADD-like behavior, combining allergic and neurotoxic reactions. It's just what it sounds like—the intestinal wall becomes excessively permeable so that food fragments get into the body that normally wouldn't. The same food fragments can be neurotoxins like the wheat proteins, which cause a direct response in the brain. Other food fragments may not directly affect the brain, but may activate the immune response because the immune system sees them as foreign invaders. Histamine and immune messenger chemicals are then released with their own powerful effects on the nervous system. Leaky gut syndrome may itself be triggered by an allergic response to a food, with inflammation of the intestinal wall. As you might imagine, these unpleasant cycles have the potential to amplify and trigger each other. An allergy inflames the digestive tract, which then leaks neurotoxins into the bloodstream and induces a secondary allergic reaction. It's a kind of negative synergy.

We can diagnose leaky gut syndrome by giving a child a special drink which contains large molecules of an indigestible sugar that normally shouldn't pass through the intestinal wall. If the sugar does get through and shows up in the urine, it's a strong sign that the intestinal wall is passing things it shouldn't. If a child shows normal intestinal permeability on an elimination diet and leaky gut when he or she resumes eating a particular food, this is also strong evidence of an allergic reaction.

If we find a child has leaky gut syndrome we definitely want to identify any food allergies that may be inducing it and eliminate the offending foods from the child's diet. We will treat a yeast infection, if there is one, since yeast can promote this condition. We can also use supplements of L-glutamine and quercetin to help restore the digestive tract.

Dysbiosis

Healthy children (and adults) support whole colonies of beneficial microorganisms in the intestinal tract; these are varying kinds of bacteria which are sometimes called the "intestinal flora." These bacteria actually help us digest our food and can process and synthesize useful nutrients for us. Repeated courses of treatment with high-powered antibiotics generally kill off much of the intestinal flora, which can then grow back in unhealthy proportions. Also, antibiotics do not kill yeast, which can take over like weeds and prevent beneficial intestinal flora from growing back. There are other causes that can also bring about an unhealthy state of bacterial imbalance in the digestive tract, a condition we call dysbiosis. This is not strictly a disease state, but a disruption of the internal environment that can take many forms. Dysbiosis can affect a child's health and behavior in multiple ways.

In one form of dysbiosis, yeast and some kinds of bacteria may produce toxins called endotoxins in the intestine that are absorbed through the intestinal wall. Some of these may affect the brain and nervous system, causing symptoms of sleep and mood disturbances. Some children may suffer from this kind of intestinal toxicity due to the overgrowth of candida or harmful bacteria. Especially if they have poor liver function, some children may have a diminished capacity to process these toxins. Some children may actually be "drunk" on the toxins, through a kind of autointoxication. Certain microbes may literally ferment sugar into alcohol, while others may break it down into toxic aldehydes. Both processes can create profound fatigue since alcohol and aldehydes stress the whole system, particularly the liver. Some of these microbial byproducts may induce an allergic reaction, while others may act as neurotransmitters in the brain. This process can vary from individual to individual since everyone carries around their own unique balance of gut bacteria. One child may literally get "drunk" from fruit juice, while another can drink it with no such effect. One child may get energized from eating meat, while another may feel as drowsy as a lion cub after devouring its share of a kill. It's interesting to note that both alcohol and aldehydes have an addictive potential, which may explain the craving/bingeing behavior of some children.

As an adult you might enjoy a shot of whiskey as an after-dinner relaxant, but you have a personality structure and psychic stability plus the awareness of the effects of alcohol to handle the temporary disturbance of your mental and physical sensations. A child who experiences autointoxication is much more susceptible, much more shaken up by the distortion of his or her perceptual world, and of course has no idea what is happening to create such peculiar feelings.

Treatment of dysbiosis, under a physician's care, may involve:

- **Changing the diet.** Some patients respond to a low sugar/ low carbohydrate/high fiber diet. Others may be helped by Elaine Gottschall's Specific Carbohydrate Diet (see next page).
- **Mineral-based detoxicants.** Bentonite, bismuth, "heil-moor" or sodium persulfate.
- **Carbohydrate supplementation** with specific compounds such as the fructose-oligosaccharides (FOS).
- **Fiber supplements** such as cellulose or psyllium.
- **Herbal anti-microbials.** Useful herbal remedies include wormwood (*Artemisia annua*), citrus seed extract, golden-seal, **Gentian** (*Gentiana lutea*) or Bloodroot (*Sanguinaria canadensis*).
- **Replenishing normal intestinal flora** with the appropriate microorganisms like *bifidobacteria, lactobacillus* and *saccharomyces boulardii*.

The Specific Carbohydrate Diet

The Specific Carbohydrate Diet developed by Elaine Gottschall goes beyond eliminating individual food allergens or even wheat gluten. Some adults and children seem to have an incomplete digestion of carbohydrates that leaves sugars and by-products in the intestine which foster the growth of harmful bacteria. These in turn release toxins into the system. The Specific Carbohydrate Diet eliminates these foods to break the cycle of overgrowth. Some carbohydrates from beans are allowed, but not soybeans, and there are no grains of any kind in this diet, not even rice. Certain starchy vegetables such as potatoes are also eliminated. See *Breaking the Vicious Cycle* by Elaine Gottschall (The Kirkton Press, Kirkton, Ontario, Canada, 1994).

Yeast: The Candida Connection

We've already mentioned it several times, but yeast overgrowth rates its own special billing among the bad actors of food reactions. One variety, called *Candida albicans*, is a living microorganism that is part of the beneficial flora that populate our bodies. Like friendly bacteria, it usually coexists peacefully with us on the mucous membranes of the throat and digestive tract. The overgrowth of yeast, a condition called candidiasis, alters the balance of the normal flora and can affect the body in many ways, resulting in allergic reactions, migraines, respiratory problems, lethargy, depression and intestinal complaints. Children may experience a worsening of symptoms after eating carbohydrates or sugar because yeast thrives on these types of foods. Many children with frequent yeast infections subsequently develop an allergy to yeast itself, with its own disturbing effects. And we've noted how yeast overgrowth can induce leaky gut and the spiraling symptoms of dysbiosis.

Candidiasis and candida allergy are treatable. Simply eliminating medicine and foods that promote yeast overgrowth are usually enough. Foods that encourage candida are:

- Sugar and refined carbohydrates.
- Dairy products.
- Fruits and fruit juices.
- Breads and yeast products.
- Antibiotic-laden meat products.

With candida infections that are deeply entrenched, a doctor may prescribe antifungal agents like Nystatin, Nizoral, Diflucan, or Sporonox.

Food Additives—The Feingold Perspective

So far I've discussed reactions to common foods. In our brave new world of processed foods, however, we eat several pounds of preservatives, sweeteners, artificial flavorings and colorings and other additives over the course of a year. We're all familiar with the effects of a food additive like caffeine, which puts the kick in high-sugared cola drinks. What we know much less about are the cumulative effects of the thousands of artificial additives in our foods, especially in children who may be uniquely sensitive to some of these.

Caffeine and drugs like Ritalin, for example, change subjective experience by working on the brain and the autonomic nervous system (the part of the nervous system that regulates bodily functions, such as breathing, sleeping, alertness and blood pressure). After taking a drug like Ritalin, a child's brain function changes as a result of the activity of neurotransmitters like dopamine and norepinephrine. One theory explains the behavioral symptoms of ADD and ADHD by suggesting that some food additives may affect some children in equally powerful ways, acting as neurotoxins or affecting normal neurotransmitter activity in the brain.

In the early 1970s, the late Dr. Ben Feingold, a pediatrician and allergist, found that he could help people who were suffering from urticaria, a condition of spontaneous rashes and hives, by putting them on a diet low in preservatives. One of the patients Dr. Feingold treated with the low-preservative diet coincidentally was suffering from schizophrenia. While on the diet not only did his hives clear up, but there was a major improvement in the schizophrenia. Based on this experience, Feingold theorized that restricting food additives might help hyperactive children, and this seemed to be borne out in his practice. He developed a diet that in particular eliminated artificial colorings, artificial flavors, the preservatives BHA and BHT, and foods and medicines containing salicylates, which include aspirin, apples, oranges and tomatoes. The Feingold diet does not restrict all processed foods, all fruits, or even sugar and chocolate. When Feingold presented his report to the American Medical Association in 1973, it raised a storm of controversy, and both the medical establishment and the packaged food industry set out to prove him wrong. A wave of studies followed of varying degrees of relevance, some purporting to show that food additives had no effect on children's behavior but others confirming that children improved on the Feingold diet. Current research is now beginning to reconsider Feingold's theory. Dr. Robert Sinaiko and others are scientifically updating it with new discoveries. Some children have been found to have a defect in an enzyme which enables detoxification of phenolic compounds. These are substances found both naturally in some foods and used as components of preservatives and food colorings. Such compounds, which include the salicylates, may have a tendency to build up in children who have the genetic enzymatic defect. They have a biochemical resemblance to some natural neurotransmitters, such as adrenaline, and may act as false neurotransmitters, triggering abnormal brain activity. Children who cannot detoxify or enzymatically convert these compounds may become overloaded to the point that their behavior is affected.

It is now possible to measure the enzymatic activity in children to identify which individuals may be more susceptible to this problem. Though not all ADHD children respond to the Feingold diet, this does not mean that the model is invalid, but rather that it applies to a specific subgroup of children who have a genetic susceptibility. The fact is, we are engaged in a huge experiment by dumping literally thousands of chemicals and additives into our food supply. While these may have been tested for safety on a limited basis, the effects when they are released into a population of millions of children are largely unknown. They may be safe and inconsequential for most children, even many children with ADD or ADHD, but they can have powerful effects on some individuals.

Detoxification Problems
While some children may respond favorably to the restriction of neurotoxic foods or additives, others may have trouble

detoxifying all sorts of substances in the body. These can include both foods and materials absorbed from the environment and natural by-products of normal metabolism. We can measure a child's detoxification capabilities with a standard test that involves giving him or her small amounts of aspirin, acetaminophen (the active ingredient in Tylenol) and caffeine. (This is a mixture equivalent to the ingredients of some common over-the-counter pain relievers.) We can then track these three different substances as they go their different ways through the detoxification pathways of the liver, and spot weaknesses.

Some children have weak detoxification pathways that can lead to critical build-ups of toxic intermediate biochemicals which would normally be eliminated from the body. These children are constantly being self-poisoned by their inability to detoxify common substances. This can be complicated by the fact that many children labeled as ADD or ADHD are on multiple medications. Besides Ritalin, these can include Depakot, an antiseizure medication; clonidine, a high blood pressure medication; and Klonopin, a Valium-like drug, all of which can affect liver function and further compromise the detoxification process.

To help these children, we start with a dietary clean-up to reduce extraneous chemicals and additives so the body doesn't have to process them and then treat dysbiosis and any yeast overgrowth, which can also overload the detoxification pathways. We can also use L-glutamine to reduce intestinal permeability and antioxidants, glutathione and molybdenum to help the body detoxify more effectively.

ENVIRONMENTAL TOXINS

One of the more interesting cases of hyperactivity I've seen wasn't my own patient, but the patient of a colleague of mine, a holistic physician whose clinic I was visiting. It happened that on that day, we saw the most troubling case he'd ever seen. In fact, to use the term ADHD to describe this kid seemed to minimize his problem. With complete compassion for Jason and his parents, I would have to say that Jason was a holy terror. From the moment he was in the office he was in nonstop motion. He tried to throw objects at us, he grabbed the medical instruments and threw them around the room, he grabbed at my colleague's glasses and broke them. He spat compulsively. In the short period of time he was in the examining room he even broke the ophthalmoscope that was mounted on the wall.

It was not really possible to examine Jason, but one of the most telling features that his desperate mother reported was that he had a bizarre obsessive habit. He would repeatedly go under the kitchen sink, open and smell bottles of household detergents, chemicals, cleaners and solvents—all those things that you are supposed to keep away from children. He appeared almost addicted to chemicals and chemical odors, and it was unclear whether they were calming him down or psyching him up.

So far we've been looking at foods and internal toxins, but of course children are surrounded, as all of us are, with the chemical odors and residues of our industrial age from paint fumes to automobile exhaust to dry-cleaning odors. It's only been recently that the diagnosis of Multiple Chemical Sensitivity (MCS) has become mainstream, and research centers have been set up at major teaching institutions to study it. The focus has been on adults, but there is reason to believe that some children may suffer from this as well. MCS has also been called the 20th century illness, universal reactor syndrome, and environmental illness. In adults, the syndrome has a wide range of symptoms, including fatigue, listlessness and mental confusion, that could contribute to a diagnosis of ADD in a child. The chemicals that can provoke this disorder are almost limitless, from the formaldehyde in new clothing to pesticide residues, passive cigarette smoke, lacquers, plastics and more.

I have seen several children in my practice who seemed to have been affected by environmental toxins, though not to the degree experienced by some adults with MCS.

Heather had just started first grade, and was brought in by her mother, Janis, who as it happened, was a schoolteacher in her child's school. Janis, who herself suffered from some chemical sensitivities, noticed that her colleagues were sick a lot of the time and suspected that the school itself was a "sick building." It was not a new school, but a lot of remodeling had gone on; new carpeting was installed, the school was newly painted and the ventilation system was always breaking down. Janis observed that a high percentage of children in the school were diagnosed with ADD, and she was concerned about her daughter. Heather had some behavioral problems at home, but her biggest problem was that she didn't seem to engage fully at school.

To see if there might be an allergic component to this, we tested Heather with an extract of "schoolroom air." Air samples from the school were collected over a period of time, using a special compressor, in order to produce a concentrate of whatever toxic elements might be present in that space.

It turned out that Heather had a profound allergic response to the school's air. This was the beginning of a major controversy at the school, as parents and teachers got together to ask the school to deal with the "sick building" issue. Meanwhile, we tried managing Heather's diet and nutrition to help her, but in the end Janis gave up and put Heather in a private school, where in fact she did much better. Now, this is not proof positive that environmental pollutants caused Heather's problem because clearly there were a lot of factors at play. The private school was certainly more sensitive to parents' concerns, and Heather's mother was clearly invested in the environmental explanation. Since she saw herself as chemically sensitive, she may have subliminally transmitted some of her expectations and responses to the child. But the fact remains that there was a startling improvement in Heather's behavior at the new school.

Heavy Metal Toxicity

Heavy metals like lead and cadmium are among the most poisonous by-products of the industrial revolution, and children are particularly vulnerable. Lead poisoning can cause impairment in perception, learning, memory and problem solving. Studies have shown that levels higher than 10 micrograms per deciliter of blood can affect mental performance, even though up to 25 mcg/dl is considered "acceptable" according to federal guidelines. Higher levels of lead have been linked to aggressive, hyperactive and violent behavior and to decreased IQ performance. There is incontrovertible evidence that lead can have an impact on ADD and ADHD-type behavior, though it may be one among several causes.

Lead poisoning is common in poverty-stricken inner-city areas because of the many old buildings with peeling lead-based paint. This is aggravated by years of pollution from cars and trucks with leaded gasoline. But children from suburban and middle- or upper-class homes are also frequently exposed to lead. Home renovations, especially if they drag on for months or years, may also be a source of exposure.

Lead is not the whole picture, either. Tests have shown that high levels of cadmium correlate with mental and behavioral problems similar to those caused by lead. Cadmium is a highly toxic chemical used in many electrical and mechanical appliances, batteries, rubber and plastic, insecticides, photograph materials and semiconductors. It is common in all industrialized countries, yet doctors do not routinely test for cadmium.

Mercury is another long-established neurological toxin, historically responsible for "Mad Hatter's Disease," found among English hat makers in the 19th century who used mercury to cure their felt. Exposure to mercury is less common in young children, since its main source is mercury-based dental fillings, but kids can absorb it by eating large amounts of tuna. I saw one child who inexplicably had a very high mercury level in his hair and urine, had no fillings and never ate fish. When I asked Mom to open her mouth, rows of gleaming silver fillings appeared, suggesting that the child's exposure most likely occurred *in utero*. Further, Dad was an avid fresh-water fisherman, and both parents consumed a lot of fish from a large inland lake that had a fair amount of industry and shipping on it. They had perhaps not heeded the local warning that pregnant women should eat no more than one fish a month from this source.

The standard treatment for lead and heavy metal poisoning is to use some kind of chelating agent to remove the metal from the blood. This can be an oral chelating agent such as Succimer or intravenous chelation in a clinical setting using an agent called EDTA. In fact, my first experience with chelation therapy was in my medical training, when I did a rotation in pediatrics at an inner-city hospital. We had an ongoing lead treatment program with a whole roomful of kids with IVs, bouncing on their beds. For mercury we can use chelation as well, and we can use natural agents including N-acetyl cysteine, glutathione, selenium and chlorella, a blue-green algae, to assist detoxification.

Hormone Disruptors

We are only now beginning to get a picture of another potential environmental factor that may affect children's behavior and mental performance. For some time scientists have been aware that very tiny amounts of pollutants like dioxins and PCBs have an "estrogenizing effect" on tissue—that is, they have an effect similar to an excess of the natural hormone estrogen. In a very real sense, we can say that our whole environment is becoming estrogenized by these pollutants, sometimes called xenobiotic compounds, xenoestrogens or hormone disruptors. So far the focus has been on their effect on sexual hormones and on how chemicals like polychlorinated biphenyls and DDT residues may change crocodile mating habits in the Everglades.

Recently, however, zoologist Theo Colborn, coauthor of *Our Stolen Future,* has raised a new alarm about the impact of synthetic chemicals. Colborn maintains that low-level contamination with these neurotoxic and endocrine-toxic compounds can interfere with thyroid hormone function in mothers-to-be, causing neurological impairment in the embryonic brain and resulting in a susceptibility to developmental problems, learning disabilities, attention problems and hyperactivity. This is cutting-edge research. We don't know the full implications, but it suggests that the increases in diagnosis of ADD and ADHD may have a partially environmental basis.

SPECIAL NUTRIENT NEEDS: THE ORTHOMOLECULAR MODEL

The Food and Drug Administration surely intended only good by publishing so-called Recommended Daily Allowances for certain vitamins and nutrients. Even if some would argue with the figures and amounts, the notion that everyone requires a minimum amount of these nutrients is a plausible one. Unfortunately, there are at least two hidden assumptions behind the RDAs that are neither plausible nor defensible. These are 1) Everyone has the same minimal requirements, and 2) Everyone requires only the listed nutrients. The fact is, people can vary widely in their nutrient requirements, and these can change over time and circumstances even in the same individual. There are also individuals who have weak or incomplete metabolic pathways who may require supplementation with nutrients that most people don't need.

Orthomolecular medicine is a big word coined by the Nobel prize-winning scientist Linus Pauling to refer to a fairly simple concept: some persons may have special needs for nutrients in order to function normally. In some cases this may be because of dietary deficiencies. In others, some ADD and ADHD-labeled children may suffer from weak nutrient pathways or may lack key catalysts for metabolic activities which in turn affect their behavior and concentration; the good news is that these weak metabolic processes can be boosted with appropriate nutrients. For example, an individual child may suffer a weakness in a pathway supported by vitamin B6, so might need "extra" B6 beyond the amount most people require for normal functioning. This is simply a matter of biochemical individuality on the molecular level—a variation from the metabolic norm.

There are virtually infinite numbers of these pathways. We can identify many through careful blood tests of nutrient levels and amino acids. Some of these appear to affect brain chemistry. There are some autistic children who respond to B6, for example, and some children with learning disabilities who respond to another B vitamin called dimethylglycine.

The testing we do is really an initial evaluation. If we test a child and find "normal levels" of a nutrient they may still have a deficiency because they need more than normal levels. Some researchers believe that we have lapsed into a false sense of security in thinking that we have effectively eradicated vitamin deficiency. Though we don't see clear cases of classical nutritional disease such as scurvy, pellagra and beriberi, we may be seeing symptoms of fragmented patterns of nutritional disease in children with ADD and ADHD. They may have borderline or individual deficiency syndromes that require special treatment.

Thiamine Deficiency and Nervous System Imbalance

Research into the effects of thiamine (vitamin B1) deficiency has offered startling insights into the relationship between nutrient needs and behavior. It's been shown that deficiencies of thiamine can affect the functioning of the autonomic nervous system. It's the autonomic nervous system that makes us sleepy and relaxed after a big meal so the digestive system can do its work. It's the same system that jolts us awake when we sense a sudden shock or danger, speeds up our heart rate and pumps blood away from the stomach and into the large muscles of the legs so that our body is prepared to fight or flee.

The classic example of a thiamine deficiency disease is beriberi, which involves neurological symptoms and a speeded-up heart rate that can lead to congestive heart failure. In a less dramatic form, Dr. Derrick Lonsdale has shown thiamine deficiency to be related to abnormal psychosomatic behavior patterns in children and adolescents and to neurotic behavior in adults.[7] These effects may be more pronounced in some susceptible children who may have earned the label of ADD or ADHD. There are children who rapidly alternate between lethargy and hyperactivity who can respond to fairly high doses of thiamine in the neighborhood of 100 mg twice daily to 500 mg twice daily. They appear to have an individualized deficiency that simply requires more thiamine to drive the weak neurological pathways.

Some Other Orthomolecular Agents

Describing all the possible nutrient and metabolic pathways that can affect ADD and ADHD-type disorders is far beyond the scope of this booklet, but we can outline at least a few of the ones a good holistic or environmental physician might look at.[8]

Thiamine (B1) may be helpful, especially if there are symptoms of thiamine deficiency. These include imbalance of the autonomic nervous system with behavioral symptoms that alternate between exhaustion and listlessness on the one hand and hyperexcited behavior on the other.

Niacin (B3) may help, particularly if there are signs of skin rash or diarrhea. Niacin is one of the mainstays of traditional orthomolecular medicine and has been used to stabilize the behavior of schizophrenics and to treat depression. It should be used cautiously only under the judicious guidance of a physician, since high doses can damage the liver.

Vitamin B6 plays a role in several pathways that can reduce internal toxins. Dr. Bernard Rimland has been using B6 to treat autistic conditions with promising results. Studies have shown that B6 can increase levels of the neurotransmitter serotonin in ADHD children with low blood serotonin levels, while reducing hyperactivity.

Vitamin B12 and **folic acid** are useful in treating metabolic imbalances marked by excess homocysteine in the blood, which has been associated with mental retardation.

Dimethylglycine, another B vitamin, has been used with

some degree of success to treat autism and is also advocated by Dr. Rimland. It can also help children with ADD and ADHD because it can modulate neurotransmitters.

Inositol, a B vitamin, may be responsible for maintaining the nerve sheath and has been used in high doses of 12-15 grams a day in research in Israel to treat panic and obsessive-compulsive disorder. In smaller amounts, it may have a calming effect on children,

Magnesium deficiency in children can cause jitters, excessive fidgeting, anxious restlessness, hair-trigger physical reflexes and responses to loud sounds, muscle cramps, tics and gesticulations, migraines and headaches and learning disability in the presence of a normal IQ.

Calcium deficiency can sometimes promote hyperactivity, as well as bed-wetting. Doctors can sometimes identify calcium and magnesium deficiency by testing a specialized tapping reflex on the cheek called Chvostek's reflex. Blood tests are of course more conclusive.

Low **zinc** levels sometimes correlate with hyperactivity.

Iron deficiency is the most common nutrient deficiency in American children and adolescents. Low levels of iron can make kids listless, spacey and unable to concentrate, typical ADD behavior. By contrast, children with high iron levels may be aggressive, excitable, oppositional and hyperactive, displaying typical ADHD behavior.

The **Essential Fatty Acids (EFAs)** are present in cold-water fish and fish oils and in some vegetable sources such as flaxseed oil, borage oil and evening primrose oil. Some studies have indicated that some children with ADHD have an altered fatty acid metabolism. EFAs may have something to do with brain development. Deficiencies are associated with dry skin and hair, excessive thirst, frequent urination, eczema, allergies, asthma, growth retardation and delayed puberty. Children who are given frequent antibiotic treatment for ear infections may develop EFA deficiencies. Supplementation may be beneficial in some children.[9]

There are several nutrients that act as precursors for neurotransmitters:

Phosphatidylcholine, which is derived from lecithin, is a precursor to the brain neurotransmitter acetylcholine, which promotes memory and concentration. Lecithin supplementation can support this pathway.

L-Tryptophan is a building block for the neurotransmitter serotonin and has a calming effect. In 1990 it was pulled off the market after one batch was badly contaminated with a toxin, so it is no longer available over the counter in health food stores. However, it is available through a physician's prescription.

The amino acids **taurine, tyrosine** and **GABA** are all thought to have a calming effect on the nervous system.

Treating Children with Supplements

Ideally, treating children with supplements should be based on extensive testing to establish each individual child's unique nutritional profile. Still, the process involves a certain amount of trial and error. This is really no different from what psychiatrists are doing with their drug prescriptions; they try out a certain dose, adjust it as needed, or find it doesn't work and try another drug. The real difference is that while there are no tests to tell you which psychiatric drugs to use, there are tests to show such factors as which amino acids may be low.

You have to be patient when working with nutrient therapies, since different nutrients show their effects over different time periods. We try most supplements for a period of one to six weeks as we continue to evaluate the child's progress. An EFA supplement regimen, however, might take six months to have an effect.

WARNING: Nutrients and supplements like those above must only be given under the close supervision of an environmental physician or a nutritionally oriented physician. I think it would be reckless to suggest dosages here, since children vary widely in body weight and nutritional needs. A child could potentially suffer damage from haphazard experimenting with nutrients. Large doses of B6, for example, seem to engender less toxicity when combined with other nutrients like B complex and magnesium. There are some preparations that are generally available that are specifically tailored for children. One is NuThera, a product recommended by Dr. Rimland with a mixture of vitamins specifically tailored to ADD and autism. It is especially potent in B6 and magnesium.

Another approach is to start with a basic multi-vitamin designed for children. Studies of young people with behavioral and psychological problems have shown that taking a daily multi-vitamin/mineral supplement can reduce violence and antisocial behavior and improve learning ability. One study showed that a small number of children reacted with worsened behavior to a supplement containing binders and fillers to which the young people were allergic. This suggests that it's important for supplements to be given in a hypoallergenic base, especially for children diagnosed with ADD or ADHD.

HOW TO HELP YOUR CHILD

Given the potential complexity of the underlying causes of ADD and ADHD-type behavior, what should parents do? Parents undertaking alternative therapies often feel ambivalent; sometimes they despair that the nutritional or allergy treatment is taking too long or may not even work; at other times they feel like dupes of the pharmaceutical industry and the close-minded psychiatric and educational establishment. When I talk to parents sitting in my office, I can sometimes see the wheels turning in their heads with the thoughts, "Whom do I believe? How much time do I have to explore these alternatives? The clock is ticking, and we have to get this under control."

I sympathize with these parents because children with an ADD or ADHD diagnosis who are not properly treated tend to lose a lot of ground, alienate teachers and psychologists and become stigmatized. Parents I see are under great pressure to do something, and do it fast. So I generally say, let's do our initial tests, let's set up a short trial of therapy. We can try this before a child goes on Ritalin or even when a child is already taking Ritalin if the parents feel the need for this kind of security. Then if we see things changing we can introduce a drug holiday and see if the child can be stabilized without the drug.

I also see parents who feel a tremendous amount of guilt. They ask themselves, "What did we do wrong? We didn't bring our child up right. Is there something wrong with our home, with our marital relationship?" These are torturous feelings, but the fact is, their children are usually experiencing a very real imbalance in their biochemical equilibrium. The alternative explanation is very healing because it provides both parents and children with a plausible explanation for the troubling behavior and relieves a certain amount of shame and guilt. We don't want to be overly optimistic and engage in illusory thinking, but if we can treat a child without drugs, this is ultimately more satisfactory for the child's self-esteem. A child with a medication history may often have a hard time living it down.

However, it's difficult to diagnose underlying problems when a child is on Ritalin because the drug masks problem behaviors. If at all possible I like to see children before they go on Ritalin. Just as with any serious condition affecting health, I recommend getting a second opinion from a doctor who practices nutritional medicine or environmental medicine before starting a child on Ritalin. Parents might decide to use natural therapies as an adjunct to Ritalin when the drug doesn't appear to be providing satisfactory results. Alternatively, parents might plan to consult an environmental physician during one of the scheduled drug holidays, which are often taken during the summer. Instead of dreading the drug holiday, parents might consider it an opportunity to try an alternative approach. If alternative treatment brings about improvement in the child's behavior there may be no need to reinstate the drug treatment.

Taking a Proactive Approach
If you suspect or know your child has ADD or ADHD there are certain things you can do on your own to try to help your child. At home, you can try a basic cleaned-up diet of fruits, vegetables and protein that is sugar-free, caffeine-free, low in carbohydrates, and low in food additives. You might also try eliminating the two most common food allergens: milk/dairy and gluten-family grains, which include barley, rye, oats and wheat. I recommend looking at some of Dr. Doris Rapp's books, especially *Is This Your Child?* Dr. Rapp offers detailed checklists for all kinds of allergic and toxic conditions and explains elimination diets you can try at home. In addition, look at your home for potential chemical toxins or allergic factors, such as new carpets, insecticides,

dust and mold and do what you can to eliminate them or lessen their impact. Then I recommend seeking out a doctor who is a member of the American Academy of Environmental Medicine. Doctors who are members of this organization are attuned to the complex allergic, nutritional, orthomolecular and environmental considerations that can come into play with ADD and ADHD-diagnosed children. A doctor should do a complete history and physical exam and perhaps a series of tests. Typically, besides urinalysis and blood count, these might include:

- Serum ferritin screening to evaluate ability to assimilate iron.
- Thyroid profile.
- Lead screening.
- Urinary amino acids and organic acids screening.
- Yeast screening.
- Allergy testing.

If the physician identifies nutritional, orthomolecular, toxic or allergic components they can be treated with nutritional supplements, an elimination diet, allergy desensitization, or several of these approaches.

Interestingly, I have found that children with ADD or ADHD problems fairly quickly develop the sense that they are separate from their symptoms, so they stop identifying with their behavior. They know it's not who they are, and they get very encouraged when we offer them an explanation and a treatment for their condition. I see kids come in who are out of control and aggressive, but they will sit down and volunteer for the treatment, raising an arm for the next allergy challenge, sticking out the tongue for the next sublingual drop. They will be nasty, resistant, tired and cranky at times, but in their lucid moments, they seem to recognize that the therapeutic process will help them. I see a stunning level of cooperation in kids who are considered to be behavioral monsters. They will give their parents a hassle but they will follow a diet. Some survival instinct or better nature seems to prevail.

As the children start to feel better and behave better, they get positive feedback from their parents and teachers, and they really thrive on this. They identify the new regimen with feeling better and respond to people being more affectionate with them, so they become very committed.

Additional Support

While we are working on the underlying causes of ADD and ADHD-type behavior, there are other areas you can look into to support your child's progress. ADD and ADHD children often respond positively to therapeutic touching. Osteopathic and chiropractic manipulative therapy is thought to modulate the autonomic nervous system directly, but even massage is an entry into autonomic healing. Another promising approach is the use of biofeedback to enable your child to actually learn to change his or her abnormal brain wave patterns.

There are also holistic ADD/ADHD parent support groups in various parts of the country that can provide channels to alternate therapies for your child. (These groups are not connected to CHAADD, the nationwide support group that is sustained in part by financial contributions from the drug manufacturers that market Ritalin.) You should consider looking into the behavioral training options that are recommended by the psychiatric establishment—specialized tutoring, intensive behavior modification, training in social skills and parenting strategies. These are all valid approaches and can provide a child (and parents) with additional support while underlying physical problems are being investigated and addressed.

Another important area you may want to consider is to have your child's learning style evaluated. Children do not all think in the same way or learn in the same way. The noted psychologist Howard Gardener has identified a number of "multiple intelligences," and good teachers are aware that individual children may need to learn material in quite different ways. Some children who sit dully in a classroom where repetition and recitation are the norm can simply blossom when physical activity, music or drama is integrated into their learning. They may need a different channel for their physical and intellectual energy than a traditional classroom provides.

ADULT ADD

There is some controversy about adult ADD: some wonder whether it really exists or whether it's a fad diagnosis. It may have joined recovered memories of child abuse as one of those syndromes about which many professionals disagree. With adults, in some cases, their ADD or ADHD diagnosis may seem like a retroactive justification for any deviation from a consistent career path. Nevertheless, many adults will retrospectively recognize, when their own children are diagnosed with ADD, that they too may have had ADD-like symptoms in childhood. In fact, there does seem to be a genetic component to the disorder. ADD and ADHD were not recognized syndromes when most adults were children, but if they had been, some with behavioral and learning problems or inability to relax and concentrate clearly might have been evaluated in this way.

Our current picture is that ADD/ADHD symptoms can be a life-long problem. Though they may appear to lessen in puberty, no one completely outgrows them. Some children labeled with ADD or ADHD may learn to compensate well enough in adulthood, while others with more profound underlying disorders continue to have problems. Adults can suffer from distraction, difficulty applying themselves to tasks, inability to relax. Haunted by difficulties in concentrating and performing, they tend to move from job to job, make many false starts in life, and feel that they are not living up to their potential. They may be ill-suited to office and white-collar work, and seem to do better in work where they don't have to interact socially.

ADD and ADHD are difficult diagnoses to make in adults. When adults have the typical ADD or ADHD symptoms they are often misidentified as anxiety, depression or obsessive-compulsive disorder. As with children, these symptoms in adults may not be a matter of hard-wired brain circuitry but rather the result of underlying problems of allergies, food reactions, dysbiosis and neurotoxins. Adults may suffer even more from environmental or chemical toxicity, since many have experienced severe exposure over many years. The good news is that many of them can be helped by some of the same approaches to diet, allergy testing and nutritional support that are successful in children.

A LOOK TO THE FUTURE

There is a phenomenon in medicine called the Inglefinger Effect that describes the way new medications and therapeutic procedures are introduced and become part of medical practice. When researchers introduce a new practice, there is usually tremendous initial skepticism and resistance; then gradually it is accepted, then wholeheartedly embraced. Finally, the pendulum can swing toward overenthusiasm and the practice becomes a therapeutic vogue. Very clearly we have seen this occur with coronary artery bypass operations and concern about cholesterol. It used to be that doctors ignored a high cholesterol count, but now a large percentage of the population is being urged to take medications to lower blood cholesterol in spite of the fact that these medications haven't been shown conclusively to have beneficial long-term effects in everyone.

What ultimately emerges is a more balanced approach, where the excess of enthusiasm for the new practice is tempered; the practice becomes part of the medical arsenal but does not eclipse all other approaches. When this happens, people are offered more individually tailored therapies instead of the therapy that's in vogue. This is what I think we will see in the case of ADD and ADHD: Ritalin will remain one of the treatment options, but the treatments and approaches outlined in this booklet will become more common. The tempering of our enthusiasm for Ritalin is really a populist revolution, led for the most part by concerned parents and teachers and a few courageous, dissenting pediatricians and mental health professionals. Parents are applying a healthy skepticism to the pronouncements of the medical establishment on ADD and ADHD. They are becoming increasingly informed and channeling their frustration with the limited options offered them into more constructive action. And this is all to the good.

RESOURCES

Books

Breaking the Vicious Cycle by Elaine Gottschall (The Kirkton Press, Kirkton, Ontario, Canada, 1994).

The Impossible Child: A Guide for Caring Teachers and Parents by Doris Rapp, M.D. (Buffalo, NY: Practical Allergy Research Foundation, 1986).

Is This Your Child? by Doris Rapp, M.D. (New York: Morrow, 1991).

Treating ADHD Without Drugs by Mary Ann Block, D.O. (Kensington Publishing, 1996).

The Yeast Connection Handbook by William G. Crook, M.D. (Professional Books, 1996).

Organizations

ADD Action Group (A support group dedicated to nondrug alternative treatments). P.O. Box 1440, Ansonia Station, New York, NY 10023. Tel. (212) 769-2457.

Feingold Association of the United States. 127 E. Main St., Riverhead, NY 11901. Tel. (800) 321-3287.

The American Academy of Environmental Medicine. P.O. Box CN1001-8001, 10 E. Randolph St., New Hope, PA 18938. Tel. (215) 862-4544.

REFERENCES

1. "Increased Medication Use in Attention-Deficit Hyperactivity Disorder: Regressive or Appropriate?" S.E. Shaywitz, M.D., B.A. Shaywitz, M.D., Yale University School of Medicine. *JAMA*, Oct. 21, 1988—Vol 260, No. 15.
2. "Clinical assessment options for children with autism and related disorders," 1/18/96 draft, The Autism Research Institute.
3. Mark Wolraich, M.D., David Wilson, Ph.D.; J. Wade White, M.D., "The Effect of Sugar on Behavior or Cognition in Children" *JAMA*, November 22/29, 1995—Vol 274, No. 20.
4. "Children with Learning and Behavioral Disorders," by A. Hoffer, M.D., Ph.D. *The Journal of Orthomolecular Psychiatry*, Vol. 5, No. 3.
5. "Controlled trial of hyposensitization in children with food-induced hyperkinetic syndrome," by Joseph Egger, Adelheid Stolla, and Leonard M. McEwen. *The Lancet*, Vol. 339: May 9, 1992, pp. 1150-1153.
6. Ibid.
7. "Functional Dysautonomia," by Dr. Derrick Lonsdale, M.B., B.S., F.A.A.P., *Journal of Advancement in Medicine*, Vol. 3, No. 3, Fall 1990.
8. Werbach, Melvyn, M.D., *Nutritional Influences on Mental Illness*. Tarzana, CA, Third Line Press, 1991.
9. Laura J. Stevens, et. al., "Essential fatty acid metabolism in boys with attention-deficit hyperactivity disorder." *American Journal of Clinical Nutrition*, 1995; 62: 761-8.